LE CORBUSIER

The Chapel at Ronchamp

Frederick A. Praeger, Publishers · New York
Distributed in cooperation with
F. W. Dodge Corporation

BOOKS THAT MATTER

Published in the United States of America in 1957
by Frederick A. Praeger, Inc., Publishers,
15 West 47th Street, New York 36, N. Y.
All rights reserved by Verlag Gerd Hatje
Library of Congress Catalog Card Number: 57-12654
Printed in Germany

CONTENTS

PREFACE

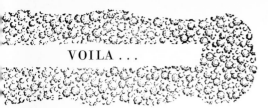

VOILA . . .

This is what slipshod, complacent language, and what the superficial mind (the shrug of the shoulders in club and salon with its «Well, why not ?») types as, «Baroque» or, should you prefer it, «Baroquism».

And from Ronchamp (1950 – 55) a retrospective judgement is made on the whole of an earnest life of struggle, of honesty, of meticulous research, of constant fight, of adjustment at every second and minute of the thousand factors which, in a true work, are all gathered and collected into a closely knit pattern – and even in the simple crossing of right angles, sign and symbol of an existence – these thousand factors about which no-one ought or would wish to speak of . . .

Painting as well as Town Planning or Architecture is involved in this verdict. (delightful, golden discovery : – «Corbu is a Baroque !»). And the figures (human) of his paintings from 1930 furnish proof of it. For the glass and the bottles of purism (a word that I did not invent myself since I was in the middle of the movement and so could not appreciate or judge it. I never had the urge, nor the right, to appraise my research or to label it) were but logic and compasses, a turning away from the confusion which . . . that . . . etc. I beg your pardon ! In 1910, I spent six weeks at the Parthenon. At the age of 23 my consciousness had determined its future direction.

«Laborious hours in the revealing light of the Acropolis. Perilous hours which brought a distressing doubt about the (real) strength of our strength, the (real) art of our art.

Those who, practising the art of architecture, find themselves at a point in their career, their brain empty, and heart broken with doubt in face of the task of giving living form to dead material, will realise the despondency of soliloquies amongst the ruins, of mute conversations with the silent stones. Very often I left the Acropolis my shoulders bowed with heavy foreboding not daring to face the fact that one day I would have to practise.

The Parthenon is a drama . . » *)

I am not faultless or simple, I am filled with turmoil and undercurrents. When pondering and working out a project (town planning, architecture or painting) always a long process, I bring into focus, I realise, I come to the point. I have made an immense effort

*) «On the Acropolis» (Travel Notebook, 1910).

without a word spoken, without speech, in the silence and solitude ; over the drawing boards of my office at 35 rue de Sèvres I do not speak ; my private office (used for patient research) at Auteuil, is opened to no-one. There I am alone. Never in my life have I «explained» a painting. The painting will go out and will be loved or hated, understood or not. Do you think that that bothers me ! (How could it bother me).

This little chapel of pilgrimage, here at Ronchamp is not a pennant marked «baroque». Reader, you do understand. I hate this term just as, in the same way I have never liked, nor looked at, nor been able to admit baroque art. An ambiguous epithet, an accusation. Modern criticism silenced by the violence of the contemporary plastic arts and aesthetics waves this garment unhooked from its cloakroom of epithets ; the bigwigs chat — to each other.

Let Ronchamp bear me witness : five years work with Maisonnier and Bona, his workmen and the engineers, all isolated on the hill . . .

Ten days before the consecration some journalists and photographers had broken the rules. They virtually machine gunned me with their flash-cameras. I told the workmen near me : «If these people don't get out of here immediately take them by the shoulders and . . .» One of these fellows who had pursued me in front of the altar of pilgrimage outside, called to me «Mister Le Corbusier, in the name of the manager of the Chicago Tribune, answer this question : Was it necessary to be a catholic to build this chapel ?» I replied «Foutez-moi le camp !».

Christmas 1956, Cap Martin

FIRST CHAPTER

les carnets de la recherche patiente

By Le Corbusier

RONCHAMP

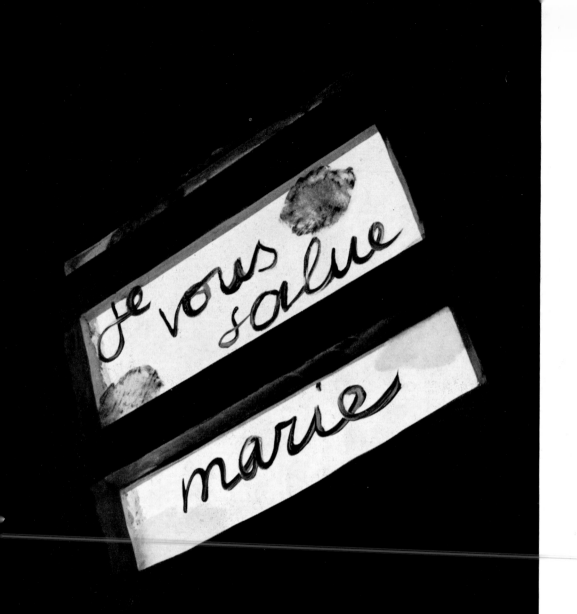

About the 30th parallel north, in the east,
the moon has a face.

In building this chapel
I wished to create a place of silence, of prayer, of peace, of spiritual joy. A sense of the sacred animated our effort. Some things are sacred, others are not whether they be religious or not. Our workmen and Bona, the foreman, Maisonnier from my office, 35 rue de Sèvres, the engineers and the calculators, other workmen and firms, executives and Savina are those who brought this project into being, a project difficult, meticulous, primitive, made strong by the resources brought into play but sensitive and informed by all embracing mathematics which is the creator of that space which cannot be described in words.

A few scattered symbols, a few written words telling the praises of the virgin.

The cross – the true cross of suffering – is raised up in this space ; the drama of Christianity has taken possession of the place from this time onwards.

Excellency, I give you this chapel of dear, faithful concrete, shaped perhaps with temerity but certainly with courage in the hope that it will seek out in you (as in those who will climb the hill) an echo of what we have drawn into it.

L-C $\frac{25}{6}$ 55

SECOND CHAPTER

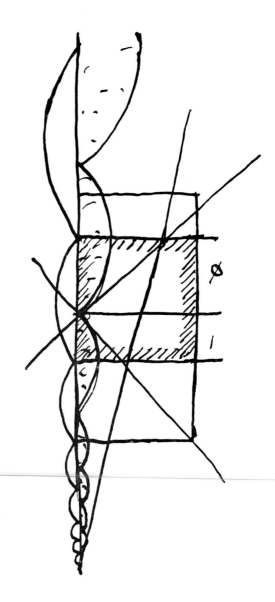

THE KEY

24
6
56

cap
martin

The key is light
and light illuminates shapes
and shapes have an emotional power.

By the play of proportions
by the play of relationships
unexpected, amazing.

But also by the intellectual play
of purpose :
their authentic origin,
their capacity to endure,
structure,
astuteness, boldness, even temerity, the play
of those vital abstractions which are the essential qualities
the components of architecture.

observez le jeu des ombres
jouez le jeu.....
Ombres propres, - nettes ou fondu
ombres portées : aigües
Ombres portées - rigueur du tracé
mais arabesque ou découpage si

ensorcelant ! Contrepoint
et fugue Musique
Grande musique !
Essayer de regarder les images
à l'envers, ou tournez-les 8 1/4.
Vous découvrirez le jeu !

serve the play of shadows, learn the game . . . Precise shadows, clear cut or dissolving. Projected shadows, sharp. Projected shadows, precisely delineated, but what enchanting abesques and frets. Counterpoint and fugue. Great music. Try to look at the picture upside-down or sideways. You will discover the game.

THIRD CHAPTER

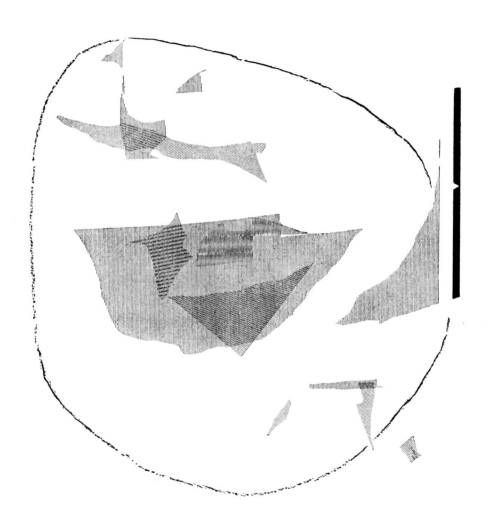

CORBU, HELP THEM

Sent by Jardot, then the manager of the Archives Photographiques de France, Mathey, today director of the Museum of Decorative Arts in Paris and Canon Lucien Ledeur from the seminary of Besançon, came to see me in 1950. Mathey: – Like Canon Ledeur I am a native of Ronchamp, a village at the foot of a hill immemorially associated with pagan and christian worship and pilgrimages. The last spur of the Vosges on the plain of the river Saône, its chapel dedicated to the Virgin, centre of devout pilgrimages it has always endured the outrages of man or the elements: lightening and wars ... the latter time and time again, during the liberation it was destroyed by artillery. For five years over-ambitious schemes have held up a solution. Corbu, go there and do a worthy job. Out of the Unité at Marseilles you made a temple to the family. Here your experience will bear on a different theme.

ONE CRAFT

In June 1950, on the hill, I spent three hours getting to know the ground and the horizons, so as to become permeated with them. The chapel, blasted by shells, is still standing. The committee is present, M. le Curé and some local contractors. I ask questions. There is no practicable road to bring transport to the top of the hill. Consequently I shall have to put up with sand and cement. Probably the stones from the ruin, cracked by frost and calcined by fire would do for fill but not for load bearing.

An idea crystallizes: here, in these conditions at the top of a lonely hill, here we must have just one all-embracing craft, an integrated team, a know-how, composed of men, up there on the hill, free and masters of their craft. Good luck!

PHENOMENON OF VISUAL ACOUSTICS

In the brain the idea is born, indefinite it wanders and develops. On the hill I had meticulously drawn the four horizons. There are only four: to the east, the Ballons d'Alsace; to the south, the last spurs leave a vale; to the west, the plain of the Saône; to the north, a small valley and a village. These drawings are missing or lost, it is they which unlocked, architecturally, the echo, the visual echo in the realm of shape. On the 4th June 1950 ... Give me charcoal and some paper ...

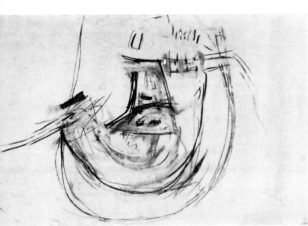 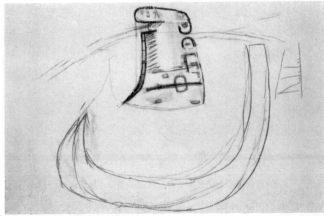

W
S —|— N
E

THE SHELL OF THE CRAB

The shell of a crab picked up on Long Island near New York in 1946 is lying on my drawing board. It will become the roof of the chapel: two membranes of concrete six

centimetres thick and 2 m. 26 cm. apart. The shell will lie on walls made of the salvaged stones . . .

To keep up the walls of salvaged stone.

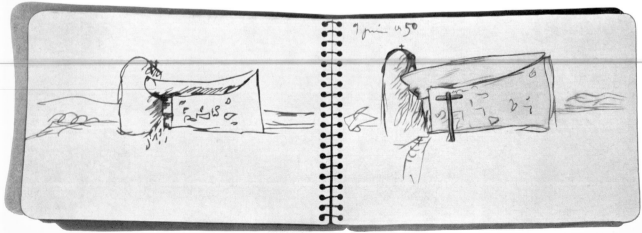

7 fermes plates
de 17 cm épaisseur
chacune différente

180
+ = 360 poutrelles
180
      27 × 5 cm
      et 4 m 30 de long
– rectilignes, standard
réalisent la toiture
en coque de <u>6 cm</u>.

Seven strong, flat beams
17 cm thick,
all different
180
+ = 360 beams
180   27×5 cm
          and 4 m 30 long.
          Rectangular, standard.
Think of the roof as a shell 6 cm thick.

LIGHT FLOWS DOWN

The shell has been put on walls which are absurdly but practically thick. Inside them however are reinforced concrete columns. The shell will rest on these columns but it will not touch the wall. A horizontal crack of light 10 cm. wide will amaze.

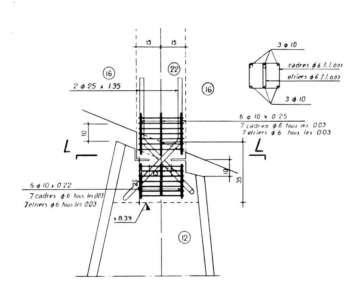

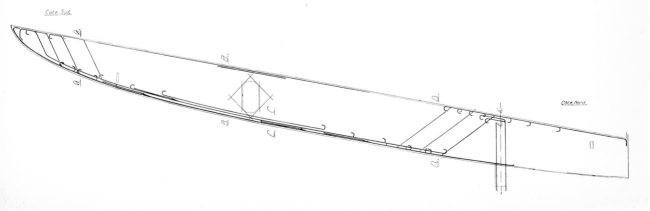

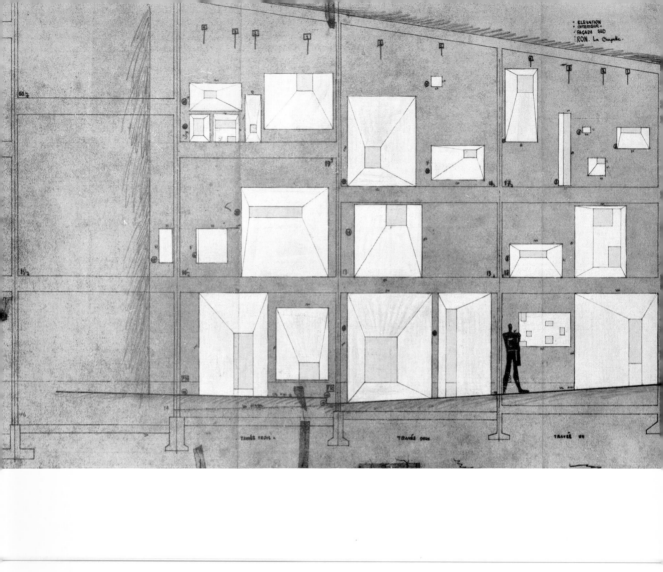

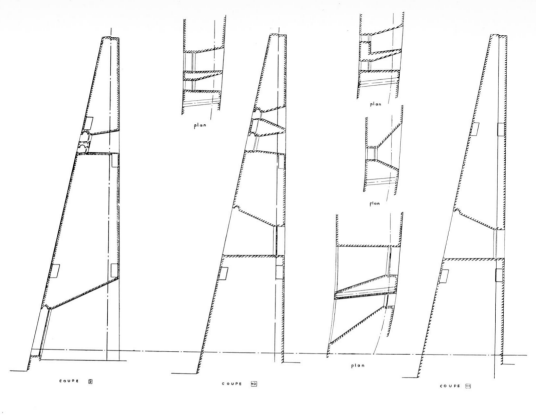

COUPE 2   plan   COUPE 10   plan   plan   plan   COUPE 11

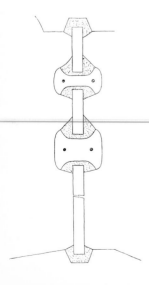

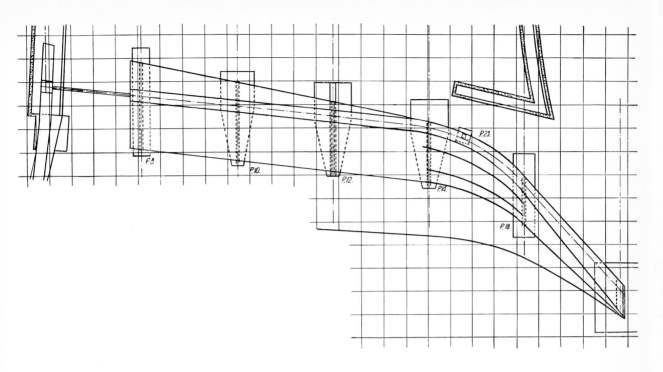

This south wall provokes astonishment. Vertical triangular frames of reinforced concrete 16 cm. thick varying, at the base, from a width of 3 m. 70 to 1 m. 40 to 50 cm. at the top, carrying the immense, spreading shell of the roof; the rest, the bays, embrasures and splays which break up the interior wall (and scarcely puncture the façade) is a membrane of concrete 4 cm. thick sprayed on to expanded metal by cement gun.

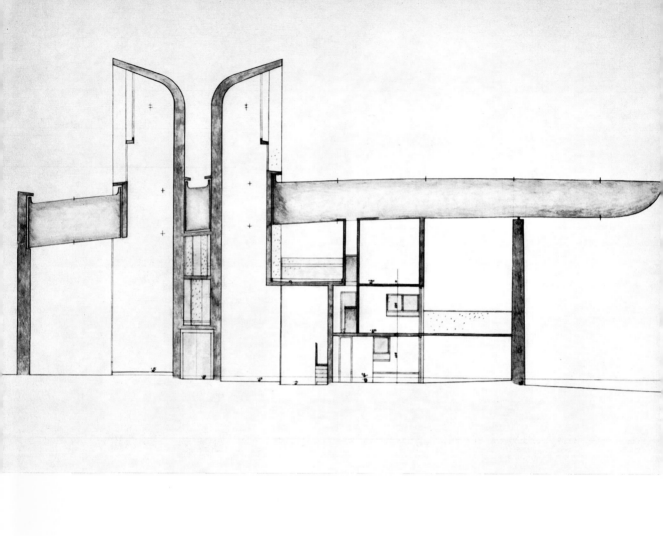

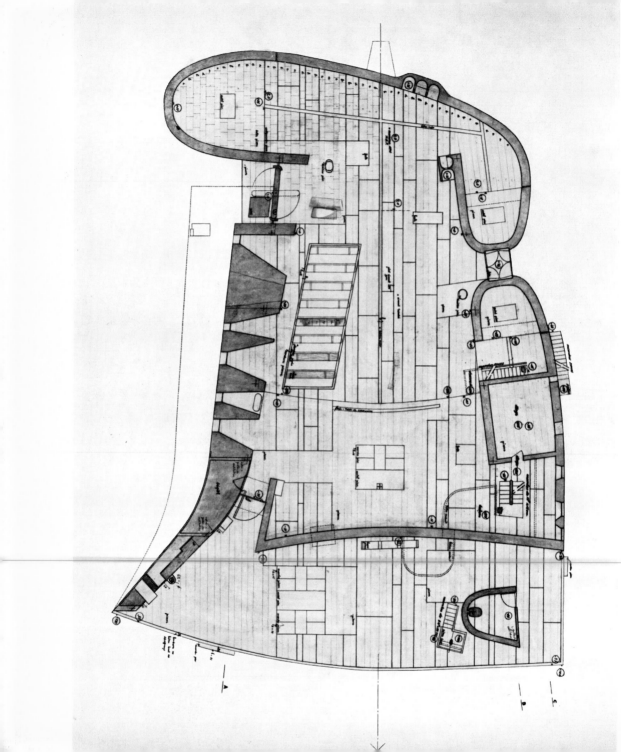

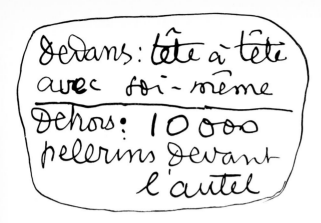

Inside, alone with yourself.
Outside, 10,000 pilgrims in front of the altar.

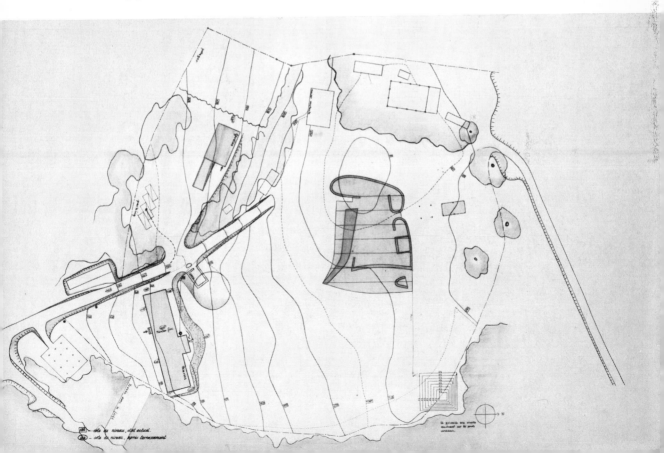

MODELS

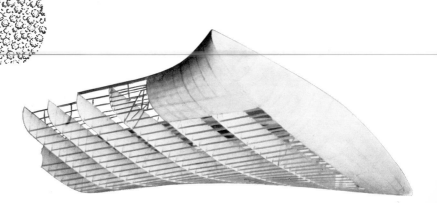

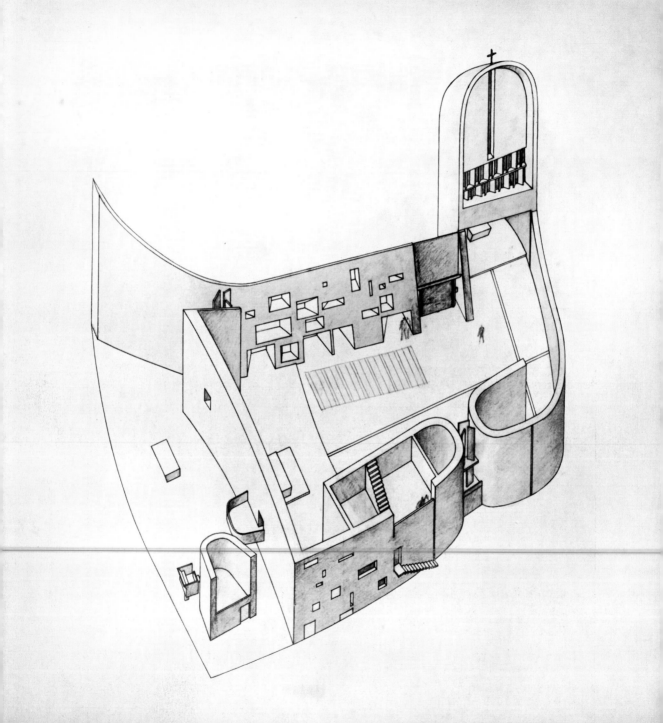

CONCERNING MATERIALS

Béton brut poured into shuttering of planks, joists sawn across, building board or ply-faced board – Cement gun – Dressed stone from Burgundy (altars) – Paving in the sacred places of stone, elsewhere of cement *opus optimum* (modulor) – Wood and *béton brut* (benches by Savina from Tréguier) wood block flooring – Cast iron (communion table, main door and railing) – *Vitrages*, and not stained glass windows – In bronze (the main processional door of bronze, enamel and cast iron) – Enamel for this door : 18 sq. metres of enamel fired at 860° C – ... and stone from the ruin – The huge trough of the roof is a shell of reinforced concrete protected by several coats of waterproofing with an aluminium sheath.

bénie

entre

toutes

MODULOR

Modulor partout

Jè défie le visiteur de mettre spontanément des chiffres dimensionnels sur les diverses parties de l'édifice

Modulor everywhere.
I defy a visitor to give, offhand, the dimensions of the different parts of the building.

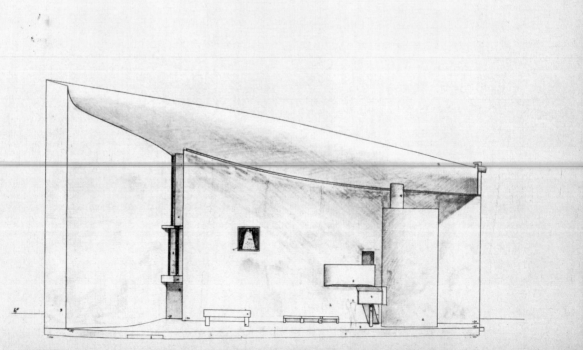

des volumes
courbes
réglés par des génératrics
rectilignes.

Curved volumes governed by rectilinear generators.

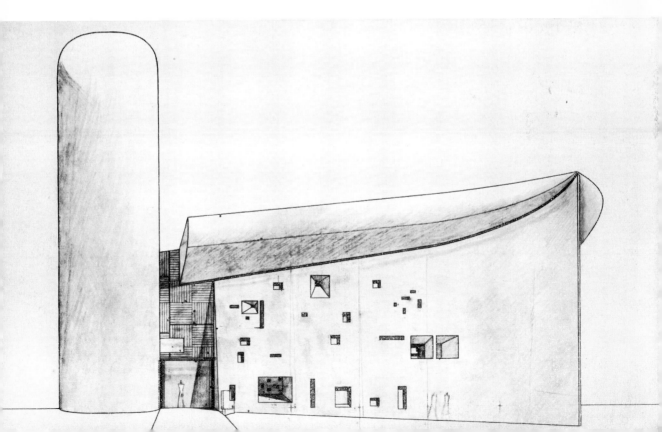

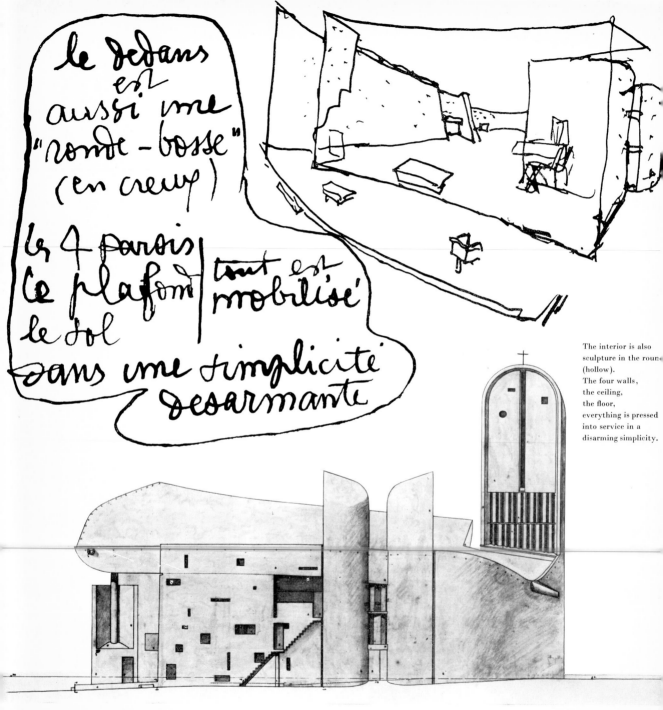

le dedans
est
aussi une
"ronde-bosse"
(en creux)

les 4 parois
le plafond | tout est
mobilisé
le sol
dans une simplicité
désarmante

The interior is also
sculpture in the round
(hollow).
The four walls,
the ceiling,
the floor,
everything is pressed
into service in a
disarming simplicity.

S.V.P!
(encore plus bas)!

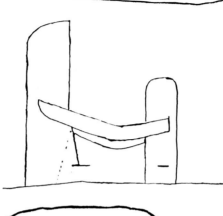

Here 4 m 52 high equals twice 226 cm.

$ici =$ **4m 52 de haut** $= 2 \times 226$

Surface BB1 joins up with surface A, A 1, A 2, A 3
like the curve of a rising wave.

A .... A₁

B   B1

"ici"

façade ouest

A2 façade est   A3

La surface
BB1
se raccorde
à la
surface
A, A, A₂ A₃
comme
une
onde
croissante

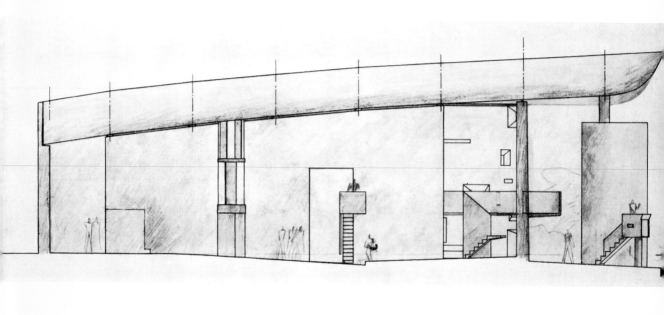

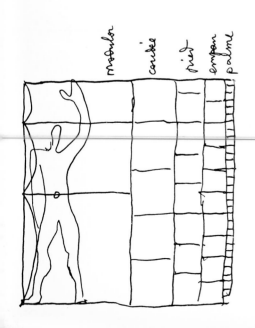

módulo
caribe
fris
empan
palm

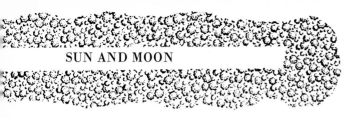

SUN AND MOON

Sun, moon, birds, the convex pentagon, the starry pentagon – clouds, sea, meanders, windows and two hands . . .

Birds sometimes have four wings it all depends on their flight. Look, observe! Having discovered it for myself one day I have recently noticed that Byzantine archangels (and others still older on the Euphrates) also have four wings.

Abstract art which, rightly, nourishes so many passions in these days is the raison d'être of Ronchamp, the language of architecture, plastic equations, symphony, music or numbers (but devoid of metaphysics) the compass needle pointing to that space which is beyond written description.

I was telephoning – the photograph of the reredos by Boulbon was in front of me upside down. The pentagon hit me in the eyes . . .

I trace the working drawing but the edges of the sheet are obliterated by the printing mask of the photographer. I call Jardot on the phone, I get a proof without mutilation. All the internal harmony of the work is in the drawings. This has been so since the loftiest and most ancient cultures. It is incredible that artists – today – should be indifferent (even hostile) to this prime mover, this «scaffolding» of the project.

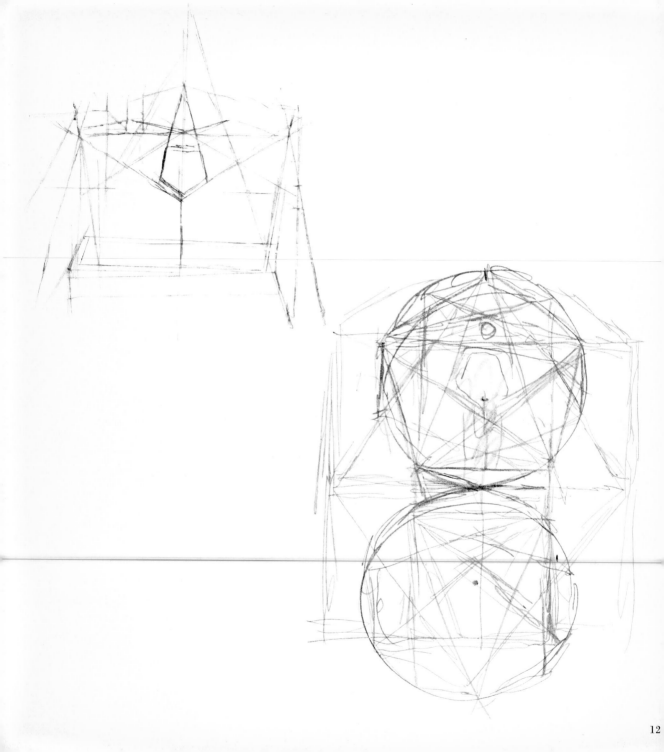

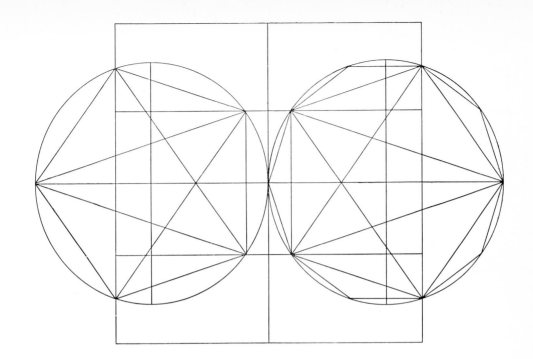

CONCERNING MEN

Lord Bishop Dubourg of Besançon visits the office, 35 rue de Sèvres. Claudius Petit is present. The first model is there. Five years later Lord Bishop Dubois consecrates the chapel.

The spur : Canon Lucien Ledeur of the Seminary of Besançon, a native of Ronchamp. The real awakener : R-P Couturier of Paris, now dead. An unshakeable committee ! Alfred Canet at Ronchamp, Carraud the lawyer at Vesoul.

Firm and unruffled till the next ice age, upright, loyal, faithful, devoted to his profession : A. Maisonnier, for 10 years architect in the office at 35 rue de Sèvres. He dashes to his drawing board and to the site. He has seen everything and done everything.

The other one is Bona from Trévise, the foreman, the tamer of the team isolated high on the hill : pickaxe, trowel, hammer, iron, poured concrete, masonry, cement gun . . . In the wind, under the sun and partly in winter he has realised the architects' drawings, the engineers' calculations, and «lent a hand» with his men in everything. His men : Raymond Boccalini, Mauro Orlandini, Alfred Fossier, André Guyon, Charles Cadore, Fredy Augustiniak.

The Méchinauds, the two sons and their father from up there, wrought and cast iron (dependable, strong ironwork).

Prouteau, an engineer of the Sté Nationale de Construction, and the calculations and working drawings of Gouton and many others. Mr. Randon, the director, showed great patience and courtesy.

Savina, a joiner from Tréguier (and my collaborator in sculpture) made the benches with his own hands.

The cast iron was made by the Fonderie Jean Cordonnier of Lure and the ironwork of the entrance door of the chapel by the Ateliers de Construction Métallique d'Héricourt, under the management of M. Vielard. The stone altars by the quarries of Ets. Guinet, the extraordinary waterproofing of the roof-shell by Soprema. «Vitrages» wonderfully prepared by Alazard, a craftsman in mirrors, who cut, classified, set and sealed them without a single mistake. I was able to paint these transparent windows in two days at the works of Boussois at Bobigny. Jean Martin of the Electrical Enamelling Factory at Luynes fired the sixteen huge panels of the processional door the necessary number of times at 860° C ; the panels were then enamelled by my own hands, so facilitating the introduction of a new material into architecture : 16 sq. metres of enamel in a vital part of the building (yet how unexpected) . . . The photographers came later, some good ones amongst the atrocious ! Hervé of Paris, Iris Volkhart and Walter Faigle of Stuttgart, Marcel Lombard of Lyon, the people of Magnum, Hubmann of Vienna, Burri of Zurich, Perusset of Verdun, Moosbrugger of Zurich, etc . . . Taking over responsibility for the chapel, and regarding it as a modern tool able to open up fresh roads in a mechanistic society, are : l'abbé Ferry, le R.P. Regamey, le Chanoine Galloy, l'abbé Ball and others.

CARRYING THE CROSS

Five days before the consecration, the cross, full size, is brought in. From this moment Ronchamp ceases to be a building (a building in construction). Breaking the silence of the walls it proclaims the great tragedy that took place on a hill top long ago in the east.

When Bona put the cross on his shoulders and carried it to the middle of the nave behind the altar it was suddenly moving. So much so that the workmen, at first speechless, began to joke to avoid the catch in the throat.

THE SIGN

The symbol had to be placed in its right and proper position. Bona went up on the tower with two round pieces of wood, one 140 cm. and the other 113 cm. long. He put 113 across. Saw at 86. He put 86 across. Saw at 70. And bring 140 to 113. Put 70 across. Nail it! Then the bronze was cast.

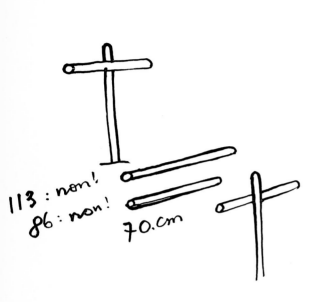

113 : non!
86 : non!
70. cm

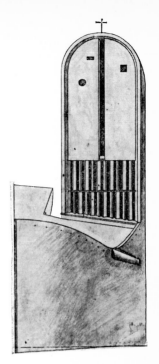

COME WHAT MAY

The work is finished.
Come what come may.

December 1956
Cap Martin

POSTSCRIPT

The positioning of the essential elements of worship in the chapel of Notre-Dame-du-Haut was temporarily settled for the dedication ceremony on the 25th June 1955.

Since then the great wooden cross fixed at the back of the altar has appeared awkward to me. I felt an increasing uneasiness about it, I concentrated on it and today, two years later, I began to draw; I made these five drawings; they are dated 25th June (just a coincidence). The drawings embody a thought which brings order, hierarchy and dignity, a thought inducing a fundamental drama. From being inert and neutral things they become active, stirring and significant.

In this way the drama is unfolded, is played and is comprehended.

This focussing is an act of architecture, an act having a real relation to architecture . . . architecture which puts all in order and regulates.

Paris, 26 June 1957

L–C

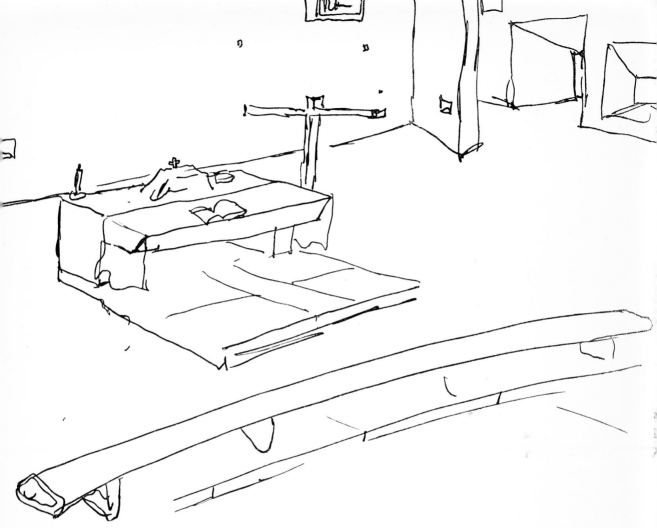

The Protagonists.

      The consecration of the host is performed on the altar

      under the sign of the cross placed on the tabernacle

      dominating the axis which commands

      the architectural arrangement of the building.

But, close by and obliquely sited, upright and full size is the witness,

      the Tree, upright, standing alone and embedded in the ground.

A= le témoin
B: le signe

The same hierarchy.

    Here, on the other hand, the priest conducts the service facing
the congregation.

Hierarchy.

      1. The sign of the cross on the axis.

      2. The witness (the Tree).

      3. The presence of the Virgin Mary.

      Side by side happily in the scheme.

The protagonists are apparent,

clearly visible, they are not confused on an opposing axis.

During pilgrimages the witness bears witness.
It bears witness to the most savage tragedy
that ever took place.

Pilgrimage.
The witness is there facing the lawn covered
with men and women
beside the altar
where the consecration of the host is about to be celebrated again.
The protagonists are there.
The presence of the Virgin Mary over the countryside and nave
the altar and the sign,
the witness.
The word will come from the pulpit.

THIS BOOK, AND ITS JACKET, ARE DESIGNED BY LE CORBUSIER

ACKNOWLEDGEMENT TO PHOTOGRAPHERS

Charles Bueb, Pulversheim (Haut-Rhin)   92 (left)

René Burri, Uetlibergstrasse 135, Zürich   8 (bottom), 109

René Groebli, Morgentalstrasse 115, Zürich   127

Lucien Hervé, 11, Rue Soyer, Neuilly-s./Seine   1, 12, 30, 31, 32, 33, 34, 35, 36, 37, 38, 39, 40, 42, 43, 44, 45, 46, 47, 48, 49, 50, 51, 52, 53, 54, 55, 56, 57, 58, 59, 60, 61, 62, 63, 64, 65, 66, 67, 68, 69, 70, 71, 72, 73, 74 ,75, 76, 78, 79, 80, 81, 82, 83, 84, 85, 93, 94, 99, 104 (top), 105, 107, 108, 110, 114, 117

Franz Hubmann, Wittegasse 8, Wien 13   16, 17, 20, 21, 22, 23, 77, 111, 112

Marcel Lombard, 56, Cours Franklin-Roosevelt, Lyon   14, 115

A. Maisonnier, Vitry sur Seine   91, 92 (right), 97, 98, 104 (bottom)

Bernhard Moosbrugger, Gemeindestrasse 25, Zürich 32   18, 19, 29

Iris Verena Volkart — Walter Faigle, Hackländerstrasse 37, Stuttgart O   13, 15, 41, 113, 116